Gideon Tibbetts Ridlon

Contribution to the Genealogy of the Burbank and Burbanck

Families

In the United States

Gideon Tibbetts Ridlon

Contribution to the Genealogy of the Burbank and Burbanck Families
In the United States

ISBN/EAN: 9783337116040

Printed in Europe, USA, Canada, Australia, Japan

Cover: Foto ©ninafisch / pixelio.de

More available books at **www.hansebooks.com**

CONTRIBUTION

TO THE

GENEALOGY

OF THE

BURBANK AND BURBANCK

FAMILIES,

IN THE UNITED STATES.

By G. T. RIDLON, Genealogist.

SACO, ME.:

FROM THE PRESS OF C. P. PIKE.

1880.

A CONTRIBUTION TO THE GENEALOGY

OF THE

BURBANK FAMILY

IN THE

UNITED STATES OF AMERICA.

———————————

NOTE. — This little work makes no pretention to be a complete genealogy of the BURBANK FAMILY from its settlement in America to the present time; it preserves such records and incidents relating to the family as could be gathered from Town and Parish Registers and by a considerable correspondence. It is to be hoped that some one will in future supply the deficiencies, and publish a complete genealogy and history of this distinguished family. No doubt errors will be discovered, but the compiler has carefully transcribed originals placed in his hands. A few blanks are inserted for corrections and addenda.

———————————

THE SURNAME. I have carefully examined the new "Doomsday Book" and can find the surname "*Burbank*" but once in a list of some ten thousand names of land-owners in Great Brittain. But I find the name "*Bowerbank*" in several counties. The name was spelled "*Borebancke*" in the early New England records. The name "*Bowbank*" is also found in English books. An old lady connected with the Long Island branch believes her ancestors spelled their names "*Burbancke*." Almost every surname found in New England has been changed in orthography, and I have little doubt that the original of this surname was "*Bowerbank*."

———————————

COAT OF ARMS. I can find no mention of a coat of Arms in "Burk's General Armory." Walford in his "County Families" does not mention the family. The tradition that they were of German derivation may be true, and if so, a coat of arms may have been granted the family before their settlement in England.

BURBANK FAMILY RECORDS.

1 **John Burbank** was made freeman in Rowley, Mass., 13 May 1640. In his will of 5 April 1681, he mentions wife *Jimima* and children *John, Caleb and Lydia*. This John is supposed to be the ancestor of all of the name in New England.

2 **Joseph Burbank** came over in the ship "Abigail" from London, England, in 1635, aged 24, but "it is not known (says Savage) where he sat down." When at the Custom House his name was spelled "*Borebancke*."

3 **Caleb Burbank**, supposed to be son of John (1) was of Rowley, Mass., in 1691. Had children John and Lydia: perhaps others. It will be seen that "*Caleb*" as well as other early family names have been continued in the family.

4 **John Burbank**, supposed to be son of John (1) was of Haverhill, Mass., and married 15 Oct. 1663, Susanna, daughter of Nathaniel Merrill. He removed to Suffield in 1680 with several children. Wife died in Suffield in 1690; and though he had second and third wives, no more children.

5 **Lydia Burbank,** daughter of Caleb (**3**) married Abram Foster in 1655.

6 **John Burbank**, son of John (**4**) married Mary Granger 21 Dec. 1699: died in 1739. See "Early Puritan Settlers of Connecticut." John's children as follows:

i. **John,** son of John (**6**) was born 18 Feb. 1701; married Rachel Austin in 1732 and had issue seven children as follows:

1 THEADORE, son of John (**i**) was born in 1733; died in 1751.
2 JOHN, son of John (**i**) was born in 1734; died in 1741.
3 RACHEL, daughter of John (**i**) was born in 1737; died 1741.
4 MARY, daughter of John (**i**) was born in 1739.
3 EBENEZER, son of John (**i**) was born in 1741.
6 JOHN, son of John (**i**) was born in 1743.
7 DANIEL, son of John (**i**) was born 1744.

ii. **Abram,** son of John **6**; born 8 Sept. 1703; married Mehitable Dwight and died Nov. 20, 1772. His children were as follows:

1 MEHITABLE, daughter of Abram (**ii**), born July 28, 1729.
2 ABRAM, son of Abram (**ii**) married 1st about 1764 Bethia Cushing of Situate, Mass., by whom one child. He married 2ndly 26 Dec., 1770, Sarah Pomeroy of Northfield, Mass., (she was born June 17, 1744), by whom he had eight children, of whom hereafter. He was a graduate of Yale College, and a successful legal practitioner. He died Aug. 8, 1808; his 2nd wife died Dec. 25, 1808. Children:

i. FRANCIS, eldest son of Abram (2), born in 1765, was married to Alexander Walcott of Windsor, Conn., and died leaving issue.

ii. ROWLAND, second son of Abram (2), born June 15, 1772, married and had a son George, now (1878) in Boston, Mass., and a daughter who collected records of many families of Burbank. Rowland died in 1845.

iii. JAMES, second son of Abram (2), was born March 7, 1775, and was lost at sea in 1805.

iv. ARTHUR, third son of Abram (2), was born Oct. 9, 1776; died Jan. 11, 1777.

v. SARAH, second daughter of Abram (2), was born Feb. 1, 1778.

vi. MARY, P., third daughter of Abram (2), was born Oct. 20, 1779; died July 14, 1851.

vii. ARTHUR, fourth son of Abram (2), was born Jan. 9, 1782; married Sarah Bates of Haddam, Conn., Nov. 27, 1810. He died March 28, 1839. Had issue as follows:

1 SARAH, daughter of Arthur (vii), was born Sept. 25, 1811.

2 ABRAM, second son of Arthur (vii) was born June 10, 1813; married April 13, 1834 Julia M. Brown of Pittsfield, Mass., and had issued. He was a builder and hotel keeper at Springfield. Children as follows:

i. CHARLES H., son of Abram (2), born Aug. 13, 1835; died Oct. 8, 1843.

ii. GEORGE W., son of Abram (2) was born Nov. 8, 1837; married Samantha L. Stevens of Windsor, Mass., and has issue as follows:

1 CLARISA M., born Aug. 20, 1860.)
2 JULIA L., born June 19, 1862. }
3 GEORGE A., born May 15, 1864,)

iii. JAMES A., son of Abram (2), was born Sept. 12, 1839; married Mary E. Sperry of Batavia, N. Y., and has one child. He is a shoe dealer at Pittsfield, Mass.
1 JAMES A., born 1868.

iv. MARY E. daughter of Abram (2), was born Sept. 15, 1841; was married Dec. 12, 1865 to Henry A. Smith of New York City.

v. CHARLES H., son of Abram (2), was born Dec. 29, 1843; married Dec 15, 1868, Jennie Halford Brook, of Tewksbury, Gloucestershire, England, and has issue. He is a carpenter at West Pittsfield, Mass. His children are as follows:

1 CHARLES A., born Oct. 9, 1870.)
2 ROBERT A., born Dec. 28, 1872. }
3 SARAH J., born Sept. 7, 1876.)

vi. WILLIAM P., son of Abram (2), was born April 4, 1846; married Hattie Rachel Smith, of New Lebanon, New York, Sept., 4, 1867. Hotel keeper at Pittsfield, Mass. Children as follows :
1 MARY P., born Sept. 24, 1868. ⎫
2 WILLIAM R., born Jan. 15, 1871. ⎬
3 ABRAM, born April 10, 1876.   ⎭

vii. EDWARD A., son of Abram (2) was born April 29, 1848: died Jan. 20, 1849.

viii. SARAH J., daughter of Abram (2), was born Jan. 4, 1850: was married March 21, 1871 to William W. Lamb of Albany, N. Y., and had issue.   He died Dec. 15, 1871.

ix. ROLAND E., son of Abram (2), was born June 1, 1852; married Margaret C. Chamberlain, of Dalton, Mass., Nov. 1, 1876 and has one child viz :
1 MINNIE P., born Aug. 30, 1877.

x. MERRICK A., son of Abram (2), was born Dec. 19, 1854.

3 HANNAH, daughter of Arthur (vii), born July 10, 1815 ; married Dec. 31, 1838, Henry C. Morse, of Enfield, Mass., who died in Chicago, Ills., Oct. 10, 1854. The widow married Dec. 18, 1856, to Hiram Hurd of Enfield, who died Feb. 27, 1872.

4 JAMES, second son of Arthur (vii), born Dec. 28, 1817, married Frances Henrietta Alesbury in Galveston, Texas, and had a daughter.   He died Feb. 18, 1861.

5 SUSANNA, second daughter of Arthur (vii), born July 9, 1821 : married May 15, 1839 to Sylvester C. Wright of Enfield, Mass.

6 THEODAH, third daughter of Arthur (vii), born Aug. 15, 1825 ; died May 6, 1877.

7 MARY P., fourth daughter of Arthur (vii), born March 30, 1828, and married Augustus W. Glines of West Springfield, Mass.

viii. THEODAH H., fourth daughter of Abram (2), was born June 28, 1783; died June 26, 1828.

ix. SUSANNA, fifth daughter of Abram (2), was born July 27, 1785 : died March 21, 1841.

3 ELEANOR, second daughter of Abram (ii); born April 4, 1734.
4 SHEM, third son of Abram (ii), was born May 21, 1736.
5 ABRAM, fourth son of Abram (ii) was born Feb. 24, 1738.
6 RUTH ,third daughter of Abram (ii), was born Aug. 26, 1741 :
7 ANN.

iii. **Joanna**, eldest daughter of John (6), was born Aug. 19, 1705.

iv. **Mary,** second daughter of John (6), was born May 26, 1707.

v. Timothy, third son of John (6), was born Aug. 1, 1709; married E. Hackett, 1732, and had issue as follows:
1 SYBBEL, daughter of Timothy (v), born 1734; died 1741.
2 ASHBEL, daughter of Timothy (v), born 1737, died 1741.
3 ESTHER, daughter of Timothy (v), born 1739; died 1741.
4 SYBBEL, daughter of Timothy (v), born 1741.
5 ASHBEL, daughter of Timothy (v), born 1745.

vi. Caleb, fourth son of John (6) was born Aug. 16, 1716.

7. Eleazer Burbank, son of John (4) and his wife Mary Granger, married Rebecca Prichard in 1690, and had issue as follows:

i. Ebenezer, eldest son of Ebenezer (7), born 1700; died at Hanover, (?) in 1722.

ii. Samuel, second son of Ebenezer (7), born in 1702, died 1723.

iii. Thankful, eldest daughter of Ebenezer (7), born in 1704.

iv. Ann, second daughter of Ebenezer (7), born 1707; died 1710.

v. Caleb, third son of Ebenezer (7), born 1712, died same year.

vi. Noah, fourth son of Ebenezer (7), born in 1713.

vii. Daniel, fifth son of Ebenezer (7) born in 1719.

BURBANKS OF VERMONT AND NEW HAMPSHIRE.

(ROWLEY BRANCH.)

8 Nathaniel Burbank was born (probably in Massachusetts) 1748; married Mary —— (who was born in 1754, and died Sept. 11, 1733) and had issue. He lived in Vermont. Died in Vermont Oct. 13, 1841. Undoubtedly some some one will know the parentage of this Nathaniel. His children were as follows:

1 **Betsey,** daughter of Nath'l (8), born 1778; married —— Johnson; died Sept. 24, 1835.

2 **Nathaniel,** son of Nath'l (8), born in Sanbornton, N. H., Feb. 25, 1782; married Sally Adye, Dec. 4, 1810, (she was born at Hartford, Vt., April 24, 1782) and had issue as follows:

i. ANSEL, born in Walden, Vt., Aug. 13, 1811, and married Betsey Adye, of Napoli, N. Y., Jan. 6, 1852.

ii. ANN, born in Walden, Vt., Nov. 13, 1812; married Jan. 27, 1846 to William Slocum of New York.

iii. Hiram, born in Cabot, Vt., Jan. 9, 1814; married Ann Eliza S. Cram of Napoli, N. Y., Sept. 27, 1841.
iv. Emerline, borne in Cabot, Vt., Jan 10, 1816; married William Adye of Napoli, N. Y., Dec. 8, 1482.
v. Rowena, born in Cabot, Vt., Nov. 26, 1817; married Fred. Williams of Napoli, N. Y., Feb. 9, 1858.
vi. Charles, born in Perry, N. Y., Aug. 4, 1819; married Elizabeth W. Hewett, of Napoli, N. Y., Aug. 4, 1849.
vii. George, born in Perry, N. Y., June 5, 1822; married Nancy Bell of Napoli, N. Y., Aug. 24, 1847.
viii. Olive, born in Napoli, N. Y., April 16, 1825; married Lorin Boardman, May 6, 1850.
ix. Austin, born in Napoli, N. Y., Jan. 24, 1827; married Fanny Hatch, April 9, 1857.
3 William, son of Nathaniel (8), was born in Sept. 1790; died Sept. 10, 1833.
4 Polly, daughter of Nathaniel (8), was born in 1800; married —— Nichols and died Jan 23, 1842.
5 Sally, married —— Eddy and died in 1852.
6 Joseph, died in Vermont.
7 John, died in Vermont.
8 Jacob, died in Vermont.
9 Moses, died in Vermont.

BURBANKS OF NEW HAMPSHIRE AND MAINE.

(ROWLEY BRANCH.)

9 Eleazer Burbank, born in Bradford, Mass., in 1708; married 1st Miss Raugh by whom he had one son. He married 2ndly Mercy Baily (she was born in Bradford, Mass., Feb. 1802) and had issue several children of whom hereafter. Eleazer had five brothers viz: *Moses* of Boscowan, N. H.; *John*, whose son Caleb settled in Windham, N. H.; *Abraham* settled in Maine, and *Daniel* in Worcester, Mass. See other families mentioned in this book.

1 Ezra, eldest son of Eleazer (9) married a Miss Plummer and had issue as follows:
i. Anna, who married Burpe, or Burley.
ii. Huldah.
iii. Eunice, who married —— Cate of Allenston, N. H.
iv. Enoch, who married —— Jennes) of Rye, N. H.
v. Lydia died unmarried.

2 **Abner**, second son of Eleazer (9), (eldest by 2nd wife) was born in Bradford, Mass., Feb. 1737; married Elizabeth Hale and had issue four sons and one daughter of whom hereafter. Resided in Bradford and Rowley, Mass., Kingston, N. H., Newfield, Me. He died in Tuftonboro, N. H., with his son *Jonathan* subsequent to Feb. 29, 1813. His wife Elizabeth died in Newfield with her son *Samuel*, after her husbands decease. Children as follows:

i. HALE, who lived in Alexandria, N. H. Drowned in fording Androscoggin river. Had one son *John*, who sometime lived in Brighton, Me.

ii. Hon. JONATHAN, resided in Tuftonboro, N. H., (He was a Governor) had one son and nine daughters, named as follows: *Abner*. A daughter married —— Richardson and lived in Tuftonboro, N. H. One daughter married —— Severance. *Ruth*, married —— Chase. *Sally*, married —— Neal. *Eunice*, married Mr. (afterwards Gen.) Hoyt of Centre Harbor, N. H.

iii. BETSEY, only daughter of Abner (2), married —— Berry and lived in Canada.

iv. SAMUEL, third son of Abner (2) was born in Rowley, Mass., April, (?) 1769; married Susan Graves of Poplin, now Fremont, N. H., (she was born in Brentwood, N. H.) and had issue thirteen children, of whom hereafter. He died in Newfield, Me., Sept. 3, 1832, aged 67 years, 7 months. He was Town Clerk and Selectman in Newfield, many years. His wife died Jan. 14, 1853, aged 77 years. Children as follows:

1 Rev. SAMUEL, eldest son of Samuel (iv), was born in Brentwood, N. H., June 17, 1792; married Nancy, daughter of Dea. Joseph Drew, (she was born in Newfield, Me., Dec. 5, 1803) Dec. 3, 1822, and had issue seven children, of whom hereafter. He was 30 years in the Gospel ministry — Free Baptist. Was one of the founders and original proprietor of the "Morning Star" a religious paper first issued in Limerick, Me., May 11, 1826. He was Treasurer of York County about eight years. Trustee of Parfield Academy. Was first settled F. Baptist preacher in Newfield, Me. Chairman of Selectmen in 1821. Died in Limerick, Me., Sept. 24, 1845. Children:

i. MARTHA A., born in Newfield, March 5, 1824; married James M. Woodman, (F. W. Baptist Minister), Aug. 2, 1847, and died at Mt. Pleasant, Wis., Aug. 22, 1860.

ii. MARY, born in Newfield, Jan. 22, 1826; died in Limerick, April 22, 1827.

iii. OLIVE J., born in Limerick, June 8, 1827; died Sept. 2, 1830.

iv. ARTHUR C., born in Limerick, Nov. 29, 1832; married
Lucy Hoyt, of Vermont, Oct. 11, 1859.

v. CHARLES H., born in No. Berwick, Dec. 8, 1835; died
at Mt. Pleasant, Wis., March 15, 1860.

vi. JOSEPH D., born in Limerick, March 27, 1838; died
there Nov. 12, 1860.

vii. MARY J., born in Limerick, Nov. 18, 1841; married
Oct. 12, 1871, Benjamin R. Frisbie of Kittery, and died
April 20, 1872.

2 SUSAN, eldest daughter of Samuel iv), was born in Newfield, Me., March 5, 1795; married Aug. 31, 1815, Eph-
raim G. Smith of Wakefield, N. H.; died Dec. 17, 1879,
leaving issue.

3 URSULA, second daughter of Samuel (iv), never married.

4 JOSEPH M., second son of Samuel (iv), was born in Parsonsfield, Me.; died in Wakefield, N. H., aged 20 years.

5 AMELIA, third daughter of Samuel (iv), was born in Newfield, Me.; married Alfred Woodman of Wakefield, N. H.,
and died there.

6 AMOS, third son of Samuel (iv) was born in Newfield, Me.,
Dec. 24, 1803; married Nancy Moore of Newfield, (she
was born April 20, 1808) and died in Wellington, Nevada,
Nov. 2, 1878. He once lived in Tamworth, N. H. His
widow still living. Children as follows:

i. SARAH R., born in Newfield, Me., Aug. 23, 1830; married in Chicago, Ills., in Nov. 1856 to Samuel Morris
of Ohio. Deceased.

ii. SAMUEL M., born in Newfield, Me., March 10, 1833.
married in Tamworth, N. H., Jan. 2, 1868, to Mary M.
Nickerson, (She was born May 19, 1845) and resides at
Wellington, Nevada.

iii. SUSAN J., born in Tamworth, N. H., March 26, 1836;
married Nov. 2, 1868, to N. B. Isbell of Kentucky.
He died at Empire City, Nevada, June 14, 1873.

iv. SILAS E., born in Limerick, Me., June 17, 1841.

v. JOSEPH P., born in Tamworth, N. H., April 28, 1844;
married Sept. 4, 1875, to Lizzie Kline of Virginia City,
Nevada, and lives in the West.

vi. CHARLES P., born in Tamworth, N. H., Jan. 1, 1850,
and died in Virginia City, Nevada, Sept. 30, 1876.

7 ABNER, Esq., fourth son of Samuel (iv), was born in Newfield, Me., Dec. 27, 1805; married Eliza Adams Harmon,
March 8, 1837 and had issue, of whom hereafter. He
has been much in public life. Was Representative to the

Maine Legislature in 1839 and 1840; County Commissioner from 1847 to 1851; was Selectman and Treasurer of Limerick many years; Justice of Peace and Quorum many years; School Teacher, Land surveyor; Trustee of Limerick Academy many years. Resided in Limerick since 1832. Children as follows:

i. HORACE H., Esq., born in Limerick, Oct. 27, 1837; married Elizabeth Thompson of Kennebunk, and resides in Saco, Me. He graduated at Bowdoin College. He has been County Attorney for York County, Me., and Register of Probate for same county. Now in practice of Law with John S. Derby, in Saco. Three children.

ii. ALBION, born in Limerick, Me., Dec. 25, 1839; married Miss Olive E. Thompson. Gratuated at Bowdoin College. Was admitted to the Bar. Teacher for many years in High School at Exeter, N. H.

iii. SARAH A., born in Limerick, Me., Nov. 14, 1845. Teacher for 10 years in Biddeford High School.

iv. IDA E., born in Limerick, Me., Oct. 13, 1854; married Edwin R. Perkins of Limerick.

v. CHARLES E., born in Limerick, Me., March 27, 1859. Graduated at Bowdoin College, 1880.

8 Rev. NATHANIEL, fifth son of Samuel (iv) was born in Newfield, Me., in 1807. He was preacher in the F. W. Baptist Church. Overworked himself by hard study and became demented in latter years.

9 Rev. PORTER S., sixth son of Samuel (iv) was born in Newfield, Me., March 13, 1810; married July 16, 1837, Miriam Blazo Burbank, (she was born in Newfield, Me., Jan. 22, 1812) of a kindred stock, and had issue five children, of whom hereafter. He graduated at Dartmouth College in 1837. Taught in Stafford Academy N. H., 3 years. Ordained F. W. Baptist minister, and has preached since 1840. Has been corresponding Editor of the "Morning Star" 30 years. Clerk N. Hampshire Yearly Meeting 6 years. President F. W. B. Educational Society several years. Trustee of New Hampton Seminary, N. H., Maine State Seminery at Lewiston and Bates College. Now resident in Parsonsfield, Me. Children:

i. ELIZA A. S., born in Parsonsfield, Me., Oct. 30, 1838; died Aug. 25, 1839.

ii. MEHITABLE F. B., born in Parsonsfield, Me., June 10, 1840; married May 13, 1859, to Henry S. Wharton, of Huntingdon, Pa.

iii. PORTER M., born at Hampton, N. H., Aug. 15, 1842; married S. Emma White of Exeter, N. H., March, 1870.

iv. MIRIAM E., born at Hampton, N. H., Aug. 6, 1846;
married Nov. 5, 1874, Joseph Daniel Conway of Portland, Me.
v. MARCIA A., born at Deerfield, N. H., Feb. 19, 1849.

10 Hon. JAMES M., seventh son of Samuel (iv), was born in
Newfield, Me., Dec. 30, 1811; married Phebe Hill (she
was born in Waterboro, Me., Feb. 14, 1811) Nov. 1,
1835, and died in Saco, Me, April 26, 1875. He was several
years a trader in Waterboro', Me. Was Representative in
Maine Legislature in 1845. Kept hotel in Sanford several
years. Sheriff of York County from 1859 to 1864. Was
Selectman and City Marshall of Saco, and State Senator.
Children as follows :
  i. CHARLES E., born Feb. 18, 1837 ; died in Sanford, Me.,
     Oct. 26, 1855.
  ii. ELLEN F., born June 29, 1840 ; married in May 1866,
      to Buel C. Carter of Ossipee, N. H.
  iii. ANN E., born March 5, 1844 ; married William C. Fox
       of Wolfborough, N. H.
  iv. EMMA, born July 26, 1852 ; married —— Webber of
      Saco, Maine.

11 HANNAH, fourth daughter of Samuel (iv), was born in Newfield, Me. Married Daniel Campbell of Wakefield, N. H.
12 ALMIRA, fifth daughter of Samuel (iv), was born in Newfield, Me. Never married.
13 LOUISA, sixth daughter of Samuel (iv), was born in Newfield, Me. Never married.

3 David, a son of Eleazer (9) lived in Deerfield, New Hampshire. No other information.

BURBANKS OF KENNEBUNK MAINE.

(ROWLEY BRANCH.)

10 John Burbank, was born in Bradford, Mass. Was one of
the first settlers in Arundel, (now Kennebunk), Me. Millman,
by occupation. Engaged in coasting trade and lost a large
schooner on his first trip to Halifax, in 1750. Was 2d Lieut.
in the expedition to Louisburg, in 1745. His wife's name does
not appear. His children as far as known to the author, as follows :
  i. John, son of John (10), was "master-at-arms," under Paul
     Jones in the "Bon Homme Richard" and the "Serapis,"
     and while the latter was sinking he released the prisoners and
     was censured by Jones ; this was during the encounter with

the "Countess of Scarborough." He was stationed at Portsmouth, in the company of Capt. Eliphalet Davis, in 1776. Was captured in the brig "Charming Polly," and sent to England on board the "Dalton," in 1777. He subsequently settled in Lyman, Me., and was living there in 1837.

ii. **Benjamin**, son of John (10), settled in Brownfield, Me. He married and had a numerous family, as follows :

1 Dea. ASA, son of Benjamin (ii), married Eunice Hutchins, 1751 ; 2ndly Esther Emery, 1767 ; 3dly Hannah Foster. Was Selectman in Arundel, (Kennebunk), in 1780. Died in Feb. 1824, aged 90. He was in the expedition to Louisburgh, or his uncle by the same name. Children as follows :

i. JOSEPH, who died at sea.
ii. CALEB, who married Sally Littlefield. Was a blacksmith in Parsonsfield, Me. Had several children. 1 *Samuel.* 2 *Esther*, married John Lord. 3 *Hannah*, married —— Merrill.
iii. ASA.
iv. RUTH.
v. ANN.
vi. JOHN D., (Colonel) married the widow of his brother David. Was Cabinet maker in Saco. Married Susan Stowell, (she was the widow before named) in 1797 ; she died in Saco in 1805, aged 36 years. He married secondly Sarah, daughter of Abijah Felch (or Fitch), of Limerick, Me., 1807. Died in 1842 aged 66 years. Children as follows :

1 DAVID, son of John (vi), was trained for mercantile persuits, in Portland, Me. When Portland became a city in 1830, he was member of the City Council. In Military affairs, familiarly known by old Portlanders as "Major." Was Brigade Inspector. Long member of the Masonic Fraternity ; now permanent member of "Grand Royal Arch Chapter" of Maine, as the records of Annual Convention show. Has held many positions of trust. Went to Baltimore, Md., in 1841. Married Sophia, youngest daughter of Samuel Andrews, Esq., (known as "Merchant Andrews") of Bridgton, Me., and is now 1880) living in Baltimore. Children :

i. ELKANAH, son son of David (1), born in Portland, Me., Aug. 1, 1824 ; died at Baltimore, Md., Oct. 11, 1848, aged 24.
ii. MARTHA H., daughter of David (1) born in Portland, Me., May 8, 1826 ; married July, 1849 to Nathan Webb, who died Nov. 3, 1865 ; he was of Cincinnati, Ohio. She was living in Baltimore in 1877.

iii. DAVID L., son of David (1), born in Portland, Me., Jan. 26, 1829; died July 13, 1868 leaving a widow and daughter *Ida* who is now (1877) in Athens, Ga. His wife's name was L. W. Hopkins of North Carolina.

iv. CAROLINE, S. daughter of David (1) born in Portland, Me., Dec. 7, 1830; died Dec. 26, 1832.

v. LEONARD, son of David (1), born in Portland, Me., Dec., 20, 1833; married Mary O. Elsenden (or Essenden) Oct. 27, 1859, and has five children, all born in Baltimore, Md., (where he resides) as follows: *Sophia*, *Kattie*, *Olivia*, *James D.*, and *Leonard A.*

2 Rev. JOHN F., son of John (vi) born in Portland, Me., and became Baptist preacher; settled in Worcester, Mass. Died in 1853, aged 42 years. His wife died in 1847 aged 34 years. Children *George L.* and *Charles.*

3 TAMSEN S., daughter of John (vi), married Capt. Hezekiah Adams, and died in Warrenton, Me., (?) in 1876 aged 76 years.

4 SUSAN, daughter of John (vi), married Samuel McLellan of Upper Stillwater, Me.

5 SARAH, daughter of John (vi) married Timothy Sedgely of New Portland, Me., and died in 1854, aged 47.

6 SOPHRONIA, daughter of John (vi), married Capt. Samuel Andrews of Bridgton, Me., and died in 1874 aged 76.

7 NANCY, E., daughter of John (vi), married Elias Berry of Bridgton, Me., in 1834 and (1877) is supposed to be living in Boylston, Mass.

8 Rev. DANIEL E., son of John (vi) was a Baptist preacher in Winthrop, Me. Died 1840, aged 26.

9 LYDIA C. daughter of John (vi), married Michial J. Merrill of Bridgton, Me., 1837.

10 HARRIET R., daughter of John (vi), married —— Bithers (?) of Leroy, Minnesota.

11 A. T., son (?) of John (vi), married Blackman of Worcester, Mass., 1842.

12 ASA L., son of John (vi) married Martha Barnard; now (1877) in Worcester, Mass.

13 CHARLES W., son of John (vi), married Eliza J. Phillips, of Worcester, Mass. Died 1851, aged 27.

NOTE. David Burbank, Esq., of Baltimore, Md., says he visited his grandfather, Deacon Asa, at Arundal in 1812–13, and remembers well his uncles Ebenezer and Moses; their residences were about three miles from Kennebunkport. Moses was a Sea Captain and Ship Master.

vii. JOSHUA, son of Asa (1), married Sally Mitchell.

viii. DAVID, son of Asa (1), married Susan Stowell, and died young. The widow married his brother *John* beforementioned.

ix. OLIVE, son of Asa (1).

x. EBENEZER, son of Asa (1), lived in Kennebunk.

xi. MOSES, son of Asa (1) was a Ship Master. Lived about three miles from Kennebunkport, Me.

BURBANKS OF BOSCOWAN, NEW HAMPSHIRE.

(ROWLEY BRANCH.)

---

11 **Samuel Burbank,** supposed to have been born in Massachusetts, had a son.

i. **Samuel,** born Aug. 30, 1745; married Eunice Pettingill (she was born July 31, 1747: and died Jan. 4, 1837), and settled in Boscowan, N. H., when he died Sept. 3, 1819. Had twelve children as follows:

1 SAMUEL, son of Samuel (i), born Jan. 15, 1770; died Oct. 29, 1772.

2 JOSEPH, son of Samuel (i), born Aug. 23. 1771. Drowned.

3 EUNICE, daughter of Samuel (i) born May 2, 1775.

4 SAMUEL, son of Samuel (i), born May 25, 1777.

5 MOSES, son of Samuel (i), born Oct. 12, 1778.

6 JUDITH, daughter of Samuel (i), born Sept. 23, 1780.

7 JOSIAH, son of Samuel (i) born July 11, 1782; died June 20, 1859.

8 JONATHAN, son of Samuel (i), born April 7, 1784.

9 NATHAN, son of Samuel (i), born Feb. 24, 1786. Lived in Michigan. No issue.

10 ELIZABETH, daughter of Samuel (i), born June 6, 1788.

11 Rev. CALEB, son of Samuel (i), born Aug. 12, 1792, united with Congregational Church in 1810; labored on a farm until 21 years old when he began his preparation for College, under the instruction of the *Rev. Samuel Ward, D. D.*, of Boscowan, N. H. He entered Dartmouth College in 1817, and graduated from the same in 1821. He also completed a course of Study in the Theological Seminary of Andover, Mass., graduating in 1824. He was licensed to preach the Gospel by the Haverhill Association, and preached in New Hampshire as a licentiate more than two years. He was ordained by the Hopkinton Association in 1827, and in May of that year under the auspices of the Missionary So-

ciety of Conn., went to the "Western Reserve," Ohio. He preached at Kirtland, and Chester, Lake Co., Ohio, two years. In April 1829, he removed to Madison and Unionville, of the same County, and preached there four and a half years. While there, in 1830, he married at Kingville, Ohio, *Elizabeth Griswald Gillette*, who was born in Windsor, Conn, 1793, and with an *infant son* died the year following her marriage, at Madison, June 28, 1831, aged 37 years. On the 28 June, 1833, he married for his second wife *Miss Delphia Harris* of Florence, Ohio, who was born at Newton, Conn., Oct. 17, 1804. In March 1834, he left Madison, and preached for three years at Mesapotamia and Bloomfield, Trumbull Co., Ohio, : and at Buckville a little more than two years. While at Mesapotamia he buried *two infant daughters:* one Oct. 1834; the other July 4, 1837. In May 1840, he went to Chatham, Medina Co., Ohio, and was installed pastor of the church there by the Presbytery of Medina, and preached there 15 years, resigning his charge on account of failing health. He continued to live at Chatham until 1867, when with his wife he removed to Stamford, Del. Co., New York. His wife died April 4, 1872, and on the 5th Oct. 1856, he died, aged 84 years and nearly two months. They were both buried in the Cemetery at Stamford. They left an only daughter.

i. MARY E., only surviving daughter of Caleb (11), born at Bucksville, Ohio, June 20, 1837 ; married Rev. Leonard F. Richards, Oct. 24, 1864, and in 1817 was living at Stamford, New York. They have issue.

BURBANKS OF FALMOUTH AND SCARBOROUGH, ME.

12 **Capt. Silas Burbank,** was born in Rowley, Mass., in 1738 ; married Hannah Baird and settled in Falmouth, Me. He was probably a brother, or cousin of Deacon Asa Burbank of Arundel, Me. Was carpenter and cabinet-maker ; worked finishing the cabins of fine ships. Was an officer in the army of the Revolution ; two sons served with him as drummer and fifer four years. He removed to Scarboro' prior to 1763 ; he and wife "owned ye covenant" there 19 June, 1763. He died in the family of his son at Parsonsfield, Sept. 14, 1814, aged 76 years. Children as follows :

i. **David,** eldest son of Silas (12), born in Falmouth, Me., 1762, was in the army of the Revolution as musician at the age of 13 years.

ii. Eleazer, second son of Silas (12), was born in Falmouth, Me., 14 Oct. 1764: baptised in Scarboro' 21 Oct., 1764; married Mary, daughter of Capt. John Brackett (she was born Aug. 28, 1767) Sept. 25, 1788, and had issue eleven children of whom hereafter. He was in army of the Revolution as musician at the age of eleven. Moved to Belgrade, Me., with a six-ox-team in 1798-9. He was a farmer. Children as follows:

1 John, eldest son of Eleazer (ii), was born in Scarboro', Me., 19 June 1789, and probably died young.

2 Hannah, eldest daughter of Eleazer (ii), was born in Scarboro', 3 June, 1791; married William Newcomb of New Sharon or Industry, Me.

3 Silas, second son of Eleazer (ii), was born in Scarboro', Me., 4 Oct., 1793; married Lucretia Hersum of Belgrade, settled on a farm and had three children as follows:

i. Angeline, who married John Dunn.
ii. John, who died in New Jersey and
iii. Arvilla, who married —— Dunn. } **1390075**

4 Eleazer, Jr., third son of Eleazer (ii), was born in Scarboro', 27 Jan., 1796; married Mary Prescott of Vasselboro', Me., and lived on a farm in Waterville. Died June 19, 1873. Children:

i. Caroline A., born May 6, 1830; married James Coffin of Fairfield, Me., and has issue.
ii. Lois B., born July 19, 1832; married Albert Coffin (brother of James), of Stowe, Mass.
iii. David R., born May 12, 1834. Tobacco merchant in Kentucky.
iv. Eleazer A., born Dec., 1836; married Abby Wyman of Belgrade, Me. Tobacco trader, Owensboro', Kentucky.
v. Josiah P., born April 8, 1840; married Mary Laney of New York. Commission merchant and slate miner.

5 Mary, daughter of Eleazer (ii), never married.

6 Elizabeth, daughter of Eleazer (ii), married Phineas Tolman of Industry, Me., Living 1877.

7 Caleb, fourth son of Eleazer (ii), married Charlotte Freeman and is a lawyer in California.

8 David, fifth son of Eleazer (ii), married Mary Taylor of Henderson, Ky. Planter and tobacco merchant. Had 60 slaves before the Rebellion. A wealthy man. Six children viz: 1 *David*, 2 *Annie*, 3 *Mary*, 4 *Charles*, 5 *Hallie*, 6 *Breckenridge*.

9 Sarah, daughter of Eleazer (ii), married Joseph Hill of Belgrade, Me.

10 Ambrose, sixth son of Eleazer (ii), is a single man living in wealth in New York.

11 SAMUEL, seventh son of Eleazer (**ii**), was born Aug. 23, 1813; married Mary A., youngest daughter of Samuel A. Morse of Machias, Me., and had issue. He went to Castine, when young and studied law with Hon Elijah Hamlin of Columbia; also with Hon. Joshua Lowell of East Machias. He practiced law in company with his brother *Caleb* in Cherryfield, Me., till 1849, when he went to California in the Barque "Belgrade" with a company formed in Cherryfield and vicinity. They stopped at Rio Janero on their voyage, and soon after leaving there, a violent fever appeared among them and many died. Mr. Burbank had the fever and never fully recovered from its effects. He remained in California but a few months and went to Honolula, Hawiian Islands, where two sisters of his wife were living. He practised law at Honolula and was appointed Judge of the Police Court there. He then went to Kaloa, Kanai, and became part owner and Superintendent of a Sugar Plantation. He died suddenly May 10, 1857. Children as follows:

i. MARY A., born in Cherryfield, Me., Sept. 6, 1847.
ii. SAMUEL M., born in Cherryfield, Me., Sept. 13, 1848. To-bacco merchant, Henderson, Ky.
iii. BERTHA, born at Koloa, Island of Kanai, Jan. 9, 1853.
iv. CALEB A., born at Koloa, Island of Kanai, Sept. 24, 1854. Graduate of Brown University.
v. ROBERT W., born at Koloa, Island of Kanai, Sept. 14, 1856. Graduate of Brown University.
The widow and several children live in Providence, R. I.

iii. Samuel, third son of Silas (**12**), was born in Scarboro', Me., 2 May 1772; married Esther Boothby of Scarboro', 7 August 1792 (she was born 17 Nov. 1773: died 24 Feb. 1856), and had issue twelve children of whom hereafter. Mr. Burbank settled in Parsonsfield, Me., as farmer and blacksmith(?). Died 2 Oct., 1833, aged 62. Children as follows:

1 ELEAZER, (M. D.), eldest son of Samuel (**iii**), born 17 Sept. 1793; married 2 May, 1802, Sophronia, daughter of Wentworth Ricker of Poland Me., and had issue of whom hereafter. He took his degree at Harvard College. Practiced his profession in Poland, Me., 22 years. Removed to Falmouth, and practiced extensively there. Died March 30, 1867. A man of worth and distinction. Children as follows:

i. AUGUSTUS H., (M. D.), son of Eleazer (1), born June 24, 1822; married Elizabeth, daughter of Dr. Elias Banks of Portland, Nov. 5, 1851; (she died Jan. 4, 1869) secondly, Alice Noyes, daughter of G. P. Thompson of New Haven, Conn. He graduated at Bowdoin College, Nov. 5, 1851,

and practises his profession in Yarmouth, Me.; his place
of residence. Children:

1 ANNE, born Sept. 18, 1852.)
2 ELIZABETH R., died in infancy. }
3 HUGH E., born Sept. 11, 1874.)

ii. ESTHER, daughter of Eleazer (1), born Dec. 26, 1827;
married Nov. 13, 1872, the Hon. Samuel Page Benson,
M. C., of Brunswick, Me., who died in Yarmouth, Aug. 12,
1876.

2 INFANT.

3 NATHANIEL, second son of Samuel (iii), born 27 July, 1795;
married Rebecca —— and settled as merchant in Saco, Me.,
where he died Feb. 27, 1838. Children as follows:
   i. ESTHER, born in Saco, May 14, 1821; died Nov. 14, 1843.
   ii. MALINDA, born in Saco, March 2, 1823.
   iii. EMILY, born in Saco, Oct. 3, 1825. Deceased.
   iv. HENRY W., born in Saco, Jan 21, 1828; died Feb. 10,
       1828(?).
   v. JOHN H., born in Saco, June 14, 1829; in Boston in 1878.
   vi. EMILY A., born in Saco, March 13, 1832.
   vii. ESTHER, born in Saco.

4 ABIGAIL, daughter of Samuel (iii), born in Scarboro', Me.,
(baptised May 28, 1769), and died aged 3 years.

5 HANNAH, daughter of Samuel (iii), born in Scarboro', Me.,
8 April 1800; married —— Syms, and had issue. Residence unknown.

6 SAMUEL, third son of Samuel (iii), born 31 May 1802; married Sally Pease and lived in Parsonsfield, Me. Farmer. Died
Sept. 24, 1863. Children: 1 Charles, 2 Luther, 3 Nathaniel
an editor in New Orleans, 4 John, 5 George, 6 Emily.

7 CALEB, fourth son of Samuel (ii.), born 31 March 1804, was
drowned in the Bay of Biscay 11 march 1859. Unmarried.

8 SALLY, daughter of Samuel (iii), born 15 Aug. 1806; died
28 Dec. 1846.

9 ARCHIBALD, fifth son of Samuel (iii), born 18 July 1808,
and settled in Newfield, Me. Farmer. Died 2 Aug. 1875.
Children: 1 James, 2 Monroe, and others whose names do
not appear.

10 HARRIET, daughter of Samuel (iii), born 15 Jan. 1811;
married Elisha Piper of Parsonsfield, Me.

11 MARY, daughter of Samuel (iii), born 29 May 1813; married Silas Burbank (?) of Newfield, Me.

12 WILLIAM, sixth son of Samuel (iii), born 15 June, 1816.
Farmer in Parsonsfield, Me. Has a son and two daughters.

iv. Caleb, fourth son of Silas (**12**), was mate of a ship, and was lost at sea, aged 20 years.

v. Abigail, daughter of Silas (**12**), married Benjamin Harmon of Scarboro', Me.

vi Miriam, daughter of Silas (**12**), married Capt. Tristram Redman.

vii. Mary, daughter of Silas (**12**), married Jonathan Piper of Parsonsfield, Me., and was the mother of a superior family. Another sister married —— Hodsdon ; her name unknown.

BURBANKS OF COMPTON, NEW HAMPSHIRE.

(ROWLEY BRANCH.)

13 Gersham Burbank, born in Bradford, Mass., 23 Aug., 1734; married Anna Pearsons, (she was born in Newbury, Mass., Sept. 4, 1738, and died in New Hampshire, Jan. 9, 1818) at Newbury, Nov. 20, 1760, and died May 14, 1817. Settled in Compton, N. H., and had ten children, all of whom lived to have families; some of them very large.

i. Jonathan, eldest son of Gersham (**13**), was born in Newbury, Mass., 20 March, 1762; married Elizabeth Thurlough (she was born in Newbury, Mass., Aug. 11, 1757; died at Compton, N. H., Dec. 21, 1855), and had issue.

  1 JONATHAN, eldest son of Jonathan (**i**), born May 21, 1786.
  2 BETSEY, daughter of Jonathan (**i**), born June 10, 1784.
  3 MOSES T., second son of Jonathan (**i**), born Jan. 11, 1790; married Esther Church and had issue as follows:
    i. MOSES, born Oct. 2, 1811.
    ii. JONATHAN, born Sept. 6, 1814.
    iii. JABEZ S., born Aug. 27, 1816; died Nov. 15, 1843.
    iv. WELLMAN, born May 20, 1819; died June 5, 1852.
    v. DAVID B., born Feb. 22, 1821.
    vi. ELIZABETH, born June 15, 1823.
    vii. ALMIRA, born Oct. 29, 1825.
  4 GERSHAM, third son of Jonathan (**i**), born May 6, 1792.
  5 EBENEZER, fourth son of Jonathan (**i**) born April 23, 1794.
  6 ALMIRA, daughter of Jonathan (**i**), born Oct. 12, 1798.

ii. Ann, eldest daughter of Gersham (**13**), born in Newbury, Mass., 27 July, 1763 and married Jonathan Pearsons of Newbury.

iii. **Benjamin,** second son of Gersham (**13**), was born March 19, 1765; married Dorcas Furbush and settled in Shipton, Lower Canada, about 1800. He died suddenly while sitting in his chair some 30 years ago; his widow a few years afterwards. Children (ten in number) as follows:

1 Lucy, married D. H. Shaw of Claremont, N. H. Deceased.
2 Benjamin, married Lydia Pattie of Holdenness, N. H.
3 Dorcas, married Martin Mathews.
4 Thirsa, married George Mathews.
5 May, married Jared Willey.
6 Abijah, married Mary Willey.
7 Lovinia, married George W. Butler.
8 Furbush, married Sally Shaw.
9 David, died young.
10 Simeon, died young.

iv. **Sarah,** second daughter of Gersham (**13**), born Nov. 22, 1766, and married Oliver Cheney. Died Jan. 8, 1800.

v. **William,** third son of Gersham (**13**), born in Compton, N. H., April 27, 1769; removed to Central Vermont, married and had issue; but I have no records.

vi. **Abigail,** third daughter of Gersham (**13**), born Feb. 27, 1771; married Eleazer Burbank, her cousin.

vii. **Ebenezer,** fourth son of Gersham (**13**), born March 4, 1773; married Lucy Robins of Plymouth, N. H., 1792 (who died in 1818, aged 44 years), and had issue 13 children. He married 2ndly, Lydia, daughter of Enoch Colby, Esq., and widow of Moses McLellan, of Thornton, N. H., by whom two children. The family moved to Bloomfield, Vt., in 1820.

1 Sally, daughter of Ebenezer (**vii**), born 1793; married John J. Libbey, of Thornton, N. H., and died in Columbia, Aug. 1863.
2 Judith, second daughter of Ebenezer (**vii**), born March, 1795; died in Bloomfield, Vt., March, 1873.
3 Mary, third daughter of Ebenezer (**vii**), born 1797; married Thomas Calden (?) of Thornton, N. H., and died in Athens, Me., 1875.
4 Naomi, fourth daughter of Ebenezer (**vii**), born 1798; married Howard Blodgett of Stewardstown, Vt., and died in Canaan, Vt., Aug. 1865.
5 Lucy, fifth daughter of Ebenezer (**vii**), born Dec. 1800; married Joseph C. Currier of Bloomfield, Vt., and died there Aug. 1854.
6 Martha, sixth daughter of Ebenezer (**vii**), born 1803; married Hiram Fuller of Bloomfield, Vt., and died Dec. 1851.
7 Lydia, seventh daughter of Ebenezer (**vii**), born 1805; married John T. G. McCurdy, of Lowell, Mass., and died there in 1860.

8 EMILY, eighth daughter of Ebenezer (vii), born 1807 ; married Enoch Rodgers of Columbia, N. H., and died Dec. 25, 1875.

9 EBENEZER, eldest son of Ebenezer (vii), born 1807, (twin to Emily), and died in Bloomfield, Vt., March 1866. Single.

10 SELDON, second son of Ebenezer (vii), born March 1810 ; married Aug. 26, 1838, Fanny S. Schoff of Brunswick, Vt., and was killed by a fall in a Sawmill at Northport, Wis., in 1870. Lumber Manufacturer. Was a prominent man. Selectman, Town Clerk, Justice of the Peace, and Representative. Children as follows :

i. ARTHUR I., born April 1, 1842, and died at La Grange, Tenn., June 28, 1863. "Gave his life for his country." Member Co. A, 8th Reg. Wis. Vols.

ii. ROLLIN S., born April 14, 1844 ; married June 16, 1869. Hermie Gleason ; she died July 6, 1878. Served in Co. A, 8th Reg., Wis. Vols. Children as follows :

1 CLARENCE, born May 26, 1870.
2 ELLA, born March 17, 1872.
3 EDGAR, born Oct. 15, 1873 ; died Sept. 1874.
4 KITTYBELLE, born March 14, 1875.
Two Infants died unnamed.

iii. JACOB M., born Feb. 7, 1847. Was member of Co. E, 5th Reg., Wis. Vols., and lost his right arm near Petersburg, Va., April 2, 1865. Resides at Northport, Wis. Teacher. Married Eva C. Dillon, April 20, 1871, and has two children, viz :

1 ARTHUR I., born June 7, 1872.)
2 HENRY D., born Oct. 22, 1873.)

iv. ALBERT A., born Aug. 2, 1851. Unmarried. Resides at Northport, Wis.

v. ANNIE L., born Jan. 28, 1854 ; married Oct. 4, 1876, to Rev. J. Haw (or Ham), of Oceola Mills, Wis., where he preaches — methodist.

11 JANE, ninth daughter of Ebenezer, (vii), born Aug. 1812 ; married John T. Gillicuddy of Lowell, Mass., and died there May 1847.

12 WILLIAM, third son of Ebenezer (vii), born Aug. 1814 ; married Sarah Cook of Compton, N. H., and resides in Bloomfield, Vt. Has been a man of influence and prominence. Selectmen, County Commissioner and Justice of the Peace. Farmer by occupation. Children as follows :

i. HENRY W., born Jan. 1845 ; married Ellen M., daughter of Rev. Moses Pattee of Bloomfield, Vt., June 1867, lives on the homestead, and has two children viz :

1 C. ARDELL, daughter, born Aug. 7, 1870.)
2 J. CARL, son, born March, 1876.   )

ii. ELBRIDGE G., born 1850; died April, 1866.

iii. CLARA E., born Nov., 1852; died April, 1865.

iv. WILLIE W., born Feb. 1863.

13 NEWELL R., fourth son of Ebenezer (vii), born Dec. 25, 1816; married Elizabeth Stickney of Beverly, Mass., (she was born Feb. 20, 1821; died at Lowell, Mass., Oct., 1847) Feb. 10, 1845; 2ndly at Dunstable, N. H., June 13, 1850, Esther Hellen Fish of Fairfield, Me. She was born May 23, 1831. He was a nurseryman. Held office of sheriff. No records of issue.

14 GILMAN,)
15 IMOGENE, (?)) sons of Ebenezer (vii), both died young.

viii. **Rebecca**, fourth daughter of Gersham (13), born April 10, 1875; married John Pattee, and died July, 1812.

ix. **Alice**, fifth daughter of Gersham (13), born July 27, 1777; married Thomas Cone.

x. **Naomi**, sixth daughter of Gersham (13), born Oct., 27, 1779; married Putnam Percival, and died in 1805.

BURBANKS OF MASSACHUSETTS AND VERMONT.

(ROWLEY BRANCH.)

14 **Samuel Burbank**, was born in Massachusetts, (probably in Rowley or Bradford), in 1706. He had a son.

i. **Samuel**, son of Samuel (14), born in Woburn, Mass., 1735; married Eunice Kendall 1773 (she was born in Sherborn, Mass., 1750; died in Proctorsville, Vt., June 30, 1845), and settled in Holliston. Resided in Lexington and Fitchburgh, Mass. Was "Lieutenant" at Bunker Hill. (See Hudsons History of Lexington.) Died in Fitchburgh, Feb. 6, 1828. Children as follows:

1 LYDIA, eldest daughter of Samuel (i), born in Holliston, Mass., March 15, 1774; died June 10, 1775.

2 SULLIVAN, son of Samuel (i), born in Holliston, Mass., Sept. 2, 1776. Soldier. Died in Lexington, Sept. 30, 1862. Children as follows. 1 *Lorenzo*, 2 *Daniel*, 3 *Sidney*, Colonel in Regular Army, 4 *Orphelia*, 5 *Paulina*, 6 *Octavia*.

3 LYDIA, daughter of Samuel (i), born in Holliston, Mass., Sept. 2, 1778, and died at Ludlow, Vt., Feb. 8, 1854. Was twice married. Had children.

4 BENJAMIN, son of Samuel (1), born in Fitchburg, Mass., March 26, 1780. Farmer. Died in Augusta, Me., Nov. 1, 1868, leaving a daughter Mary who was living in Augusta in 1880.

5 EUNICE, daughter of Samuel (1), born in Fitchburgh, Mass., March 21, 1782; married —— Marshall, and died in Natic, Mass., Oct. 1867.

6 SAMUEL, son of Samuel (1), born in Fitchburgh, Mass., March 11, 1784. Lost at sea. Unmarried.

7 DANIEL, son of Samuel (1), born in Fitchburgh, Mass., Oct. 30, 1785. Killed in sham-fight in 1804.

8 TIMOTHY, son of Samuel (1), born in Fitchburgh, Mass., Feb. 3, 1788. Adopted and name changed to Kendall. Died in Farmington, July 1876.

9 KEZIAH, daughter of Samuel (1), born in Fitchburgh, Mass., April 22, 1792; married —— Spaulding and died in Proctorsville, Vt., May 6, 1876.

10 SIMEON, son of Samuel (1), born in Fitchburgh, Mass., Nov. 30, 1794. Living in St. Paul, Minn., in 1877. Several children reside there.

i. Hon. JAMES C., son of Simeon (10), born in Ludlow, Windsor Co., Vt., in 1822; died in St. Paul, Minn., June 2, 1876. In early life taught school. Established express line from St. Paul to Galena in 1851. Was a great stage owner. Owner in heavy grocery and commission store. Transported goods of Hudson Bay Company. Built first steamer that successfully navigated Red River of the north. Was President of the Chamber of Commerce in St. Paul from 1869 to 1871. Rail Road Director. President of Fire and Marine Insurance Company many years. Was President of street railway company. Served as Representative in State Legislature. He was identified with every enterprise which contributed to the growth of the city of St. Paul. A man of integrity and worth.

11 ABEL, son of Samuel (1), born in Fitchburgh, Mass. Died in Proctorsville, Vt., May 21, 1877. Merchant. Children as follows:

i. ABEL, married Almira Blood of Proctorsville, Vt., March 7, 1827, and has issue as follows:

1 AUGUSTA, born in Proctorsville, Vt., Feb. 3, 1828; married Rev. E. A. Rice, Dec. 3, 1854.

2 VELORIA, born in Proctorsville, Vt., Aug. 11, 1832; married Charles J. Fenton.

3 ALBIN S., born April 4, 1838; married Martha Howe and has issue *Almira B.* Woolen Manufacturer.

4 HENRY Z., born July 1, 1841; married Susan A. Granger, Sept. 10, 1872. Book-keeper in Boston. Has issue as follows:

i. EDITH, born Sept. 10, 1873. Twin. }
ii. EDNA, born Sept. 10, 1873; died Aug. 10, 1874. Twin. }
5 SAMUEL K., born March 15, 1844; married Nancy J. Tot-
tingham, June 19, 1872. Formerly in St. Nicholas Hotel,
New York. Now in trade at Pittsford, Vt.
6 CLARA E., born June 16, 1850.

BURBANCKS OF STATEN ISLAND, NEW YORK.

(GERMAN BRANCH.)

15 **Abraham Burbanck,** is said to have come from Netherlands
with two brothers and two sisters in the ship "Caledonia"; the
vessel was partly wrecked on the passage and one sister was
lost. They landed in New York early in the 18th century, and
Abraham settled on Staten Island; the other brothers pro-
ceeded in other directions. This branch claim to be of a
French-German stock, and there is preserved in the family a
tall clock, writing-desk, and secretary-bureau, handed down
from the ancestor, said to be quite two hundred years old. Is
it possible that *John* and *Joseph* so early in New England,
(see other branches in this book) were of the same stock? It
will be seen that *Joseph's* name at the Custom House was
spelled almost identical with this ancestor, viz: "*Borebancke.*"
I have no mention of Abrahams wife. Children as follows:

i. **Abraham,** son of Abraham (15), was born November 20,
1745, and died May 12, 1823. Children as follows:
1 ABRAHAM, son of Abraham (i), born 1780: died 1838. He
married Catherine Houghwart, and had issue as follows:
i. MARGARET, born 1806; married Nicholas Youngman.
ii. CATHERINE, born 1808.
iii. CHARLOTTE, born 1820, (by 2nd wife) married —— Mank
of Albany, N. Y.
iv. RICHARD C., born in 1822; married Catherine M. Douglas,
and had issue as follows: 1 *Margaret,* 2 *Louisa,* 3 *Emma,*
4 *Sarah,* and 5 *Catherine.*
v. GEORGE, married Catherine Relyea, and resides in Albany,
New York.
vi. JOSEPH.
vii. ANN, married George Holt of Chicago, Ills.
2 JACOB, son of Abraham (i), married Martha Gram, (?) settled on Staten Island and had issue. Numerous descendants
are now living at Tomkinsville, Staten Island, and other

towns near.   I am sorry I could not have procured a more
complete genealogy of this branch.

  i. JOCOB L., son of Jacob (2), was born on Staten Island, New
    York, and is now living at Tompkinsville, S. I.   He has
    issue as follows : 1 *Elizabeth A.*, 2 *Margaret A.*, 3 *William
    D.*, who married Susan J. ——, and has issue William D.,
    Jr., George G., and daughters whose names do not appear.
  ii. JOHN W., son of Jacob (2), was born on Staten Island, N.
    York, married and has issue.   He lives at Castleton, Cor-
    ners, Staten Island.
  iii. ANN, daughter of Jacob (2), married —— Egbert and had
    several children.
  iv. LETTIE, daughter of Jacob (2).

3 ISAAC, son of Abraham (1), had three children as follows :
  1 *Mary A.*, married Vincent Bodie ; 2 *Edward*, Sanitary
  Police, New York, and 3 *Sarah J.*

4 JOHN, son of Abraham (1), had issue as follows : 1 *Ann*, 2
  Mary, 3 *Daniel*, 4 *Henry*, 5 *John*, and 6 *Catherine*.

NOTE.—There are two Edward Burbancks and two Samuel Burbancks (father and son), living in Staten Island.   Also, numerous
descendants of the first Abraham on the female side.   The family
is the largest on the Island ; those on the North side are said to
be "too numerous to mention."